CHAKRAS AND AURAS

INCREASE YOUR ENERGY FLOW

Published by Hinkler Pty Ltd
45–55 Fairchild Street
Heatherton Victoria 3202 Australia
www.hinkler.com

© Hinkler Pty Ltd 2021, 2022

Author: Fiona Toy
Internal design: Lisa Robertson
Cover design: Maria Daley and Hinkler Studio

Images © Shutterstock.com

All rights reserved. No part of this publication may be reproduced, stored in a retrieval system, or transmitted in any way or by any means electronic, mechanical, photocopying, recording or otherwise, without the prior written permission of Hinkler Pty Ltd.

ISBN: 978 1 4889 4752 0

Printed and bound in Malaysia

CHAKRAS AND AURAS

INCREASE YOUR ENERGY FLOW

Fiona Toy

CONTENTS

Introduction 6
The energetic human body 6

The seven auric layers 8
The human aura 8
The inner layers of the aura 11
The outer layers of the aura 12
How we relate to others
through energy 14
Intention and the aura 15

Seeing and perceiving the human aura 16
Feeling the aura 16
Developing your auric vision 20

Colour in the aura 22
Aura colours and what they mean 22
White and other colours 28
Combinations of colours in
the aura 30
Placement of colours in the aura 32

Health and the aura 34
Signs of sickness in the aura 34
The benefits of aura diagnosis 37
Energy healing and the aura 37

Strengthening and refreshing the human aura 38
Strengthening your aura 40
Refreshing and cleansing
your aura 44

Chakras 46
What are chakras? 46

The inner energy of the
seven chakras 48
First chakra 48
Second chakra 50
Third chakra 52
Fourth chakra 54
Fifth chakra 56
Sixth chakra 58
Seventh chakra 60
Minor chakras 63
The chakras and our
personal growth 64
Chakras and Kundalini 72

Healing with chakras 74
The flow of energy through
the chakras 76
Focusing on balance 77
Strengthening the physical body 78
Clearing emotional disturbances 83
Harnessing the power of
the chakras 83

Seven week programme 84

Chakras and sound 90
Toning and the chakras 92
The sounds of the chakras 93

Chakra exercises and meditations 94
Chakra meditation with music 94
Breathing visualisation 95

Introduction

The energetic human body

Every cell in the human body vibrates constantly with energy, and, for centuries, mystics and healers of many cultures have accepted that the human body draws energy into it from a universal energy field. Ancient Hindu cultures recognised the chakras as the means by which the body draws this energy, and ancient texts depict multilayered energy fields around the body (known today as the aura), yet much of the science behind these energy fields is still to be explored and explained.

Many of today's scientific discoveries confirm that we are more than just our physical body, but those other aspects of ourselves that make us 'who we are' remain mysteries to science.

Energy, by its very nature, is continually moving and changing – contracting and expanding, becoming congested and releasing once more to a free-flowing stream. The energy that is around our bodies is very much a reflection of who we are and of our state of wellbeing on all levels: emotional, physical, mental and spiritual.

The information and exercises in this book are intended to provide you with a means of discovering more about yourself by understanding and using the energy fields of the human body – auras and chakras.

The seven auric layers

The human aura

The human aura is a field of energy, encapsulating the body. It constantly ebbs and flows, is forever moving and changing moment by moment, expanding, contracting and changing in intensity and vibrancy. Each individual's aura is unique – in size, colour and quality; the aura of one person can be radically different from that of another.

Rather than being a single energetic field around the body, the human aura consists of seven distinct layers. Healers and psychics who are highly sensitive to the different qualities of energy may be able to see or feel each of the layers separately. Even without this uncommon ability, having some understanding of the different roles that each level plays can give all of us greater insight into our lives, and into how our past can impact on our current health and wellbeing.

The three layers closest to the physical body are those that are most readily 'seen'. The energy of the layers further away from the body is less dense, making these layers more difficult to see and feel. Many psychics describe being able to perceive the energy of these layers, or being able to see them 'in their mind's eye' – sensing rather than physically seeing the layers.

The inner layers of the aura

The physical auric body
This is the layer of energy that is closest to the physical body – when someone begins to see auras, this is the layer that they are most likely to be observing. This layer closely follows the shape of the body and is usually uniform in its size, being 10–21 cm (4–8 inches) deep. Irregularities in the shape or colour of this band of energy can be an indication that there is an injury or problem with the physical body in this area.

The etheric auric body
People whose life is strongly focused on their body, such as dancers and athletes, will have a particularly strong etheric aura, as it is this layer of the aura that reflects the health and condition of the physical body. This layer also closely follows the shape of the physical auric body, and is approximately 5–8 cm (2–3 inches) away from the skin. Pain experienced in the physical body will be reflected by scattered energy in this layer.

The vital auric body
As the name suggests, the qualities of this layer of the aura relate to our physical vitality and liveliness – it is relevant to the amount of vigour with which we are able to approach our lives. If our energy in this layer is strong and clear, we will have good levels of physical energy, and will feel able to cope with life's demands. If we are feeling low on energy, or sluggish and run down, the energy of the vital auric body may be depleted, congested or weak.

The outer layers of the aura

The astral auric body or the emotional aura
Our energetic interactions with others primarily concern the astral auric body *(see the 'How we relate to others through energy' section)*. When we are experiencing positive feelings and feel emotionally well and safe, the colours in this auric field will typically be bright, clear and vibrant; negativity will generate darker, muddier, less vibrant colours. Imbalances in the astral auric body can mean that our emotions prevent clear thought processes and influence our decisions. When in balance, this level provides us with the sense of choice, and the ability to transform our circumstances so that they are more personally fulfilling.

The lower mental auric body
The upper and lower mental auric bodies are sometimes viewed as two aspects of a single energetic layer, with the lower level being more to do with our conscious intellectual abilities and the upper level being more to do with our 'higher' mental capabilities, of which we may be less aware. The lower mental auric body relates to our everyday intellectual capabilities and activities.

The higher mental auric body
The higher mental auric body is the layer from which we access higher intellectual knowledge, the wisdom and information available to the collective consciousness. The spark of an idea, the muse of creativity, the inspiration behind the pursuit of ideals – all these originate from this energy.

When this aura is developed through increased awareness, personal growth and creative visualisation, it can be extremely powerful in connecting with our purpose in life, and can give us a very strong and balanced perspective on our lives.

Recreational drug use impacts on this layer greatly – mental imbalances caused by drug abuse can be a reflection of damage done in this layer.

The spiritual auric body

Our connection to the divine, to our life source, to the collective consciousness, is through this auric layer. It is through this layer that we are connected to each other – and, in fact, to all living things.

In terms of energy, this layer is considered to be the most intense of all the layers. It is thought to be diffused throughout the energy fields of the body via the crown chakra. Very few people have claimed to be able to see this level of the aura.

How we relate to others through energy

Have you ever observed the mood changing drastically when a particular person enters the room? Have you ever met someone and, for no apparent reason, taken an instant dislike to them? Or perhaps you've met someone with whom you've instantly felt very relaxed and comfortable. We can gain an understanding of all these responses and feelings by learning how we relate to other people through energy.

All living things are imbued with energy, and all living things are connected by this energy. Our auras are made up of constantly flowing energy, and that energy changes according to our moods and emotions, our mental and physical state. Our auras also interact with the auras of others.

Depending on the relationship you have with the other person, your aura may be dominated by theirs, your aura may dominate theirs, your auras may repel each other, or they may blend together. In an ideal relationship, the auras of the people will blend and merge, but remain distinct, parting when the people are physically apart. In an extreme example, such as a destructive, co-dependent relationship, the auras of two people may have merged to the point where there is almost a single energy field for them. Separating on a physical and emotional level becomes much harder for these people because of this strong energy bond.

At the other end of the spectrum, someone with a particularly strong, clear aura will positively affect the auras of those around them, bringing feelings of peace, happiness and emotional strength. Many spiritual leaders are described as having a 'presence' that has a calming, soothing effect on those around them. Most people find this very attractive – this partly explains why people with this presence often develop a 'following'.

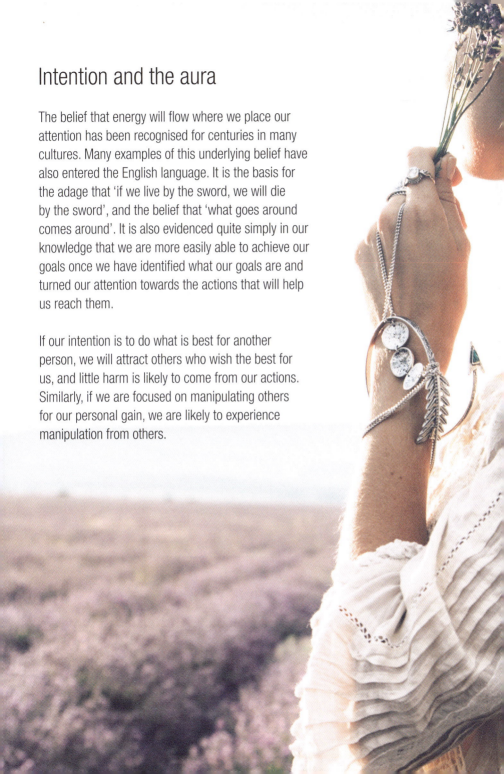

Intention and the aura

The belief that energy will flow where we place our attention has been recognised for centuries in many cultures. Many examples of this underlying belief have also entered the English language. It is the basis for the adage that 'if we live by the sword, we will die by the sword', and the belief that 'what goes around comes around'. It is also evidenced quite simply in our knowledge that we are more easily able to achieve our goals once we have identified what our goals are and turned our attention towards the actions that will help us reach them.

If our intention is to do what is best for another person, we will attract others who wish the best for us, and little harm is likely to come from our actions. Similarly, if we are focused on manipulating others for our personal gain, we are likely to experience manipulation from others.

Seeing and perceiving the human aura

A few people have always been able to see auras, without either being trained or consciously trying to develop the ability. Many people believe that children have a natural ability to perceive and see auras, but that this skill is lost as we mature and are discouraged from 'daydreaming' and living in the land of 'make-believe'. If this idea of having an innate ability to see auras is correct, it would follow that we just need to remember or 're-learn' how to perceive auras – or perhaps to allow ourselves to see auras again.

Occasionally, without any warning, a person may suddenly be able to see the colours of someone's aura and detect changes in energy fields. This can be disconcerting for the person if they are not aware that there are energy fields around our bodies, or if they are in an environment that is unsympathetic to such skills. Being disbelieved or mocked is an unpleasant experience, so there may well be many more people who can see auras than readily admit to seeing them.

Feeling the aura

Being sensitive to how energy feels and the different tactile sensations that are attributed to energy is a skill that can be developed through repetition and patience.

Your hands can become amazingly receptive with relatively little practice. We are very dependent on using visual information as our primary way of knowing the world around us; it can make it easier to focus on other senses if we have fewer visual distractions. So initially it is a good idea to practise with your eyes closed or blindfolded.

Exercise to help you feel the aura

If possible, team up with a friend who is also interested in becoming more aware of the energy fields around their body, as this allows you both to give each other feedback on what you feel.

Ask your friend to sit in a chair with their feet flat on the floor and their palms facing upwards on their thighs. Ask them to take a few deep breaths and relax.

Starting at the top of your friend's head, hold your hands about 20 cm (8 inches) away from the head, with your palms facing the person. Very slowly, move your hands around the shape of your friend's body: down around the head to the neck, across the shoulders and down the back. Then move slowly around to the front of the body. Move your hands across the front of the body and down towards the legs, then down to the feet. Take note of any changes that you feel as you move your hands around your friend's body. You may like to spend a little more time at the places where you feel a change.

Take notice of varying temperatures in the aura – you may feel places of heat or coolness, or you may notice that the energy feels 'sticky' or condensed. You may also experience places where it feels as if there are 'holes' in the energy field, or where the quality of the energy changes suddenly. As well as these more dramatic changes, you may also feel the energy change gradually from one part of the body to another. There are often quite definite differences in how the energy around the front of the body feels in comparison to the energy around the back of the body. Similarly, it is common to feel a difference in energy between the area around the head and the rest of the body.

Remember, though, that every person's energy field is unique. You may not always feel what you expect. Don't be concerned if your first attempts provide you with only a little information. It is also a normal reaction to feel that you are 'kidding yourself' that you can feel something – persevere, practise whenever you can, and you will find that your confidence and your sensitivity to energy will increase.

Developing your auric vision

Just as feeling an aura is a skill that can be developed, so the ability to see auras can also be nurtured. There are many exercises you can do to help you become able to see the energy layers of the body. The following is a fairly simple example. Remember, when you begin to attempt these exercises you may not be at all successful, or your first attempt may be less dramatic than you'd like it to be.

Exercise to help you see auras
To increase your chances of seeing the physical auric layer, softly light a room with a lamp or a small amount of natural daylight – draw any blinds or curtains against direct sunlight. Don't be tempted to use candlelight, as the flickering of the flame may create distracting shadows.

It is possible to develop your auric vision by yourself, using a large mirror so that you can view your reflection, but it is easier and more fun to develop this skill with a friend. After all, when you do first see an aura, you will want to share the good news with someone.

Ask your friend to sit in front of a plain, single-coloured background (pictures on the wall or ornaments behind your friend will be a distraction to the eye). It will be easiest at first if your friend stays relatively still or only moves very slowly during the exercise. Their aura will also be clearer and brighter if they spend a few moments in meditation before the exercise – they may choose to meditate throughout the entire exercise.

Begin by looking at a space just to the side of your friend so that you can only see their physical body in your peripheral vision, and allow your eyes to soften their focus. It is useful at this point to take a few deep breaths and try to let go of 'trying' to see colours or movement. Instead, close your eyes for a few moments and focus your intention on being open to seeing the energy fields around the body.

When you open your eyes, do not open them fully – allow your vision to remain unfocused, once again seeing the edge of your friend's physical body in your peripheral vision.

Gradually move your head so that you trace the outline of your friend's head and body with your eyes. Notice what you see. Can you detect a difference in the quality of the air around your friend's head? After a few moments, close your eyes again, and take a few deep breaths and relax.

Repeat this process a few times until you have traced the upper half of your friend's body. Don't be concerned if you do not see anything with this first attempt – simply try again later. Do be careful, however, not to tire yourself by spending long periods of time with this exercise – your best chance of seeing auric fields is when you are relaxed, not when you are fatigued and tense.

Remember that when you first begin to see the aura, what you see may be only part of what you will see after some practice. And do not be concerned if the energy you see is clear, or only has a bluish tinge, rather than the swirl of vibrant colours that practised aura-watchers can see. It is usual for colours to become more visible with practice.

> An aura dominated by reds, oranges and pinks indicates a person who is passionate about their beliefs and may act impulsively.
>
> The combination of blue, indigo and magenta in the aura suggests a person who is mentally alert and moderate in their approach to life.

Colour in the aura

Many people gifted with being able to see colour in the auric fields interpret the combinations and the position of colours in the aura of the person they are viewing. The reader of the aura may be able to gain insight into the personality of the subject, and to assess the person's attitudes, aptitudes, weaknesses and strengths. They may even be able to determine suitable career paths and goals.

Aura colours and what they mean

Colours in auras can be interpreted in many ways. It is also important to remember that your aura changes continuously, and is greatly influenced by your mood and state of health and wellbeing.

The recurrence of colours over a period of time may be a reflection of your potential or aptitude in a particular area. If you choose to develop that potential, the respective colour may change over a period of time, becoming richer and more vibrant.

Reds
Reds have long been associated with strong emotional states, such as passion, anger, lust and aggression. This association has even appeared in our use of language: the term 'to see red' means to experience a moment of blind rage. In the aura, red as a dominant colour may mean that the person's passions or strong emotions have an unhealthy predominance in their life.

In moderate amounts, red may indicate activity and stimulation – that the person is actively participating in events around them and enjoying life to the full.

Red may also indicate that the person is very comfortable with their physical body and enjoys expressing themselves physically.

Oranges
Orange is another colour that denotes activity and vitality. It is common in the auras of people who are highly motivated and who spend a significant portion of their time communicating with large numbers of people. Orange in the aura can also be a symbol of change: either recovery from an illness or injury, or transformation in one aspect of the person's life. If the orange is muddy or lacking in vibrancy, it may indicate a general lethargy – the person may need to find physical activities that they enjoy; this will help them break through their feelings of inertia and despondency.

Yellows
Yellow is the colour of intellect, so the consistent appearance of a strong vibrant sun-yellow in the aura suggests that the person is a lover of learning and enjoys the mental stimulation of new ideas, concepts and facts. A less vibrant yellow suggests either that the person is utilising their conscious mental capabilities at the present time, or that they base their decision-making on their head rather than their heart. An overabundance of yellow in the auric field may indicate that the person is very much 'in their head' – this person may not be aware of the needs of their physical body, and may not rate their feelings and emotions as being very important.

Greens

Green is the colour of balance. A green regularly appearing in a person's aura is often taken as an indication that they have a great capacity for healing and caring.

If the green is present for only a short period of time, it may be a reflection that some healing is taking place within that person – either a rebalancing of the energy fields, or some healing in the physical body, or a period of regeneration.

A muddy, drab olive shade of green, however, is not healing. This would indicate that the person may be 'green with envy', or is in some way being less than giving – they may be withholding their affection, their money or their time from someone they are jealous of.

Indigos

Indigo is indicative of the higher realms of our mental capabilities. A person with an abundance of indigo in their aura is likely to be highly intuitive and imaginative. Indigo as a dominant colour would suggest that the person leans towards having a spiritual outlook on life, and may not be motivated by the search for material things.

Violets

Violet is the colour of the higher self. If it appears strongly in the aura, the person is likely to be strongly connected to their higher values and their purpose in life. A dominance of this colour would suggest that the person is motivated by a sense of what is right. A strong sense of personal integrity will guide this person in their decision-making.

Golds
Gold is a colour of purity and of spirituality. The appearance of gold in an aura, particularly if it is the dominant colour, indicates that the person is highly evolved and lives at a level beyond the normal motivations of mere mortals. The person will almost certainly be involved in work that is for the good of humanity, and will likely be seen as a spiritual leader of some kind.

Blacks
The appearance of black in an aura is an absence of colour, rather than a colour itself. It can indicate that there is some sort of damage – either through physical or emotional trauma, or serious disease, or injury.

The abuse of recreational drugs or the extended use of very powerful prescribed drugs may also leave black 'holes' or 'gaps' in the auric field.

Whites
White is a colour of purity and of truth and wisdom. A pure white aura is rare. White may be the only colour you can see in auras initially, but a truly white aura will have a greater density of colour to it.

White and other colours

White + red
Pink as a dominant colour in the auric field indicates the presence of compassion and unconditional love. The person may have a great capacity for caring and for empathising with the needs of others. These people often choose to work with those who are generally shunned by society.

White + violet
Lavender, a mixture of violet and white, may be present in the aura of those who have psychic abilities. It is very likely that these people are able to see the colour lavender in their own auras.

Combinations of colours in the aura

Observing combinations of colours within an aura is a further step towards understanding ourselves and how the different levels of the aura interact. Psychics and mystics are likely to know intuitively the meaning of the various colour combinations, but just knowing the meaning of the basic colours gives us a key to interpreting the colours in combination. Obviously, by using this method, you may come up with more than one possibility for the colour combination.

Here are examples of just a few colour combinations and possible interpretations:

Yellow – green – orange
The following combination could indicate that the person has made a conscious decision (engaging their intellect, therefore yellow) to make certain changes for health reasons. For example, they may have chosen to follow a healthier diet and seek more exercise. These actions may be allowing the body to self-heal a number of minor ailments and conditions (healing, therefore green), and the person may be feeling inspired by the changes in their body (motivation and change, therefore orange).

Grey – black – red
This mix of colours would indicate quite different circumstances from the yellow – green – orange combination. Grey is a colour of depression, but the presence of red would suggest that there is a lot of underlying anger contributing to the depression. Black would attest to there being some form of abuse and deep hurt behind the anger.

Over a long period of time, this energy grouping would likely lead to further illness, on both a mental and a physical level.

Indigo – green – pink

This combination would be expected to be present in the aura of a powerful health carer (whether or not they were aware of their capabilities). The presence of indigo and green would mean that the person not only has a caring nature, but also has access to their intuition to help them in their work. The presence of unconditional love (expressed as pink) means that their motivation is to do the best for the people in their care.

Placement of colours in the aura

The location of colours in the aura can provide additional clues to the significance of that colour and how it relates to the person's life. Most people see the auric fields around the head and upper body first, but this does not mean that the aura does not also surround the lower body, legs and feet – it simply means that it may take a little practice and patience to be able to see it in those areas.

The head
The aura around our head tells us about our mental approach to the world, and the aura above our head reflects our spiritual nature. For example, a religious scholar may have a strong presence of yellow around the head, suggesting that the intellect is a dominant force, and violet above the head, reflecting a strong focus on the divine.

The arms and hands
The aura in this area tells us about what we are able to accept into our lives and what we are able to give. When these aspects are in balance, we are able to seek and accept assistance when we need it, and freely give what we have to others when they seek our assistance. When we are balanced in this way, the energy around our arms and hands will be clear and free flowing, with greens, blues and oranges.

The chest
The aura around our chest symbolises how we relate to those around us. It will indicate how well we are able to express ourselves and whether or not we have empathy and compassion for others. Pink in the area of the chest, for example, would suggest a person who is highly compassionate and giving.

The back
The back is symbolic of our past and our subconscious. Muddied energy in the aura at our back may suggest that we are carrying old hurts and angers with us, or that we are denying issues that are causing us emotional imbalance. Strong reds in the back may indicate that the person is holding onto anger, and is either unable or unwilling to express anger directly.

The legs and feet
The aura around our legs and feet relates to how stable our lives are, and whether we have created a solid foundation upon which to stand. If the energy in this area is sparse or not flowing freely, it may indicate that we are not 'grounded' and are prone to drift in our lives. For example, a vibrant indigo colour around the legs and feet would indicate that the person's spiritual beliefs, whatever they may be, give them stability in their life.

Health and the aura

Signs of sickness in the aura

The etheric body is the layer of the aura that gives us the most information about those imbalances which indicate disease or illness. Healers are able to pick up areas of an old sickness or illness by the quality of this layer of the auric field. Bulges, or areas where the energy feels congested or 'sticky', may indicate an area of the body which is still healing, or has been quite severely damaged in the past. Some people will be able to identify these spots by seeing or feeling the aura.

Kirlian photography and Polycontrast Interference Photography may also be able to detect illness or imbalance in the energy field. Many advocates of these systems point out that a lot more data needs to be collected before they can provide a truly accurate diagnostic system.

Many healers who are able to clearly see auric fields have also noted that the auras of people with a mental imbalance or mental illness (such as schizophrenia or bipolar disorder) are different from those of people without these illnesses. The differences are generally described as having an erratic nature to the size and shape of the energy field, and a lack of symmetry in the overall aura. Radical and fast changes of colour in the aura may also be indications of a mental health problem.

The benefits of aura diagnosis

Many healers believe that the underlying cause of any illness or disease is an imbalance of some sort in the energy field of the body, and that signs of an impending illness will appear in the aura long before there are any physical symptoms. This is one of the reasons why energy healers and orthodox medicine practitioners often disagree – energy healers believe they can pick up the very early signs of a condition, when no symptoms are occurring and there may be no sign of illness at all on a physical level. The benefit of being able to rebalance the energy fields of the body is that if balance can be restored before a physical manifestation of the illness occurs, then the illness itself may be avoided. Healing work on the aura may in fact be preventive medicine in its most effective form.

As has been seen in the powerful work of 'medical intuitives' such as Caroline Myss, the ability to sense underlying conditions that are difficult to diagnose without invasive procedures (which themselves have risks) has many benefits.

As more scientific research is carried out, and the number of doctors who advocate the healing arts increases, it is likely that energy healing and aura diagnosis will gain greater credibility and wider acceptance.

Energy healing and the aura

There are many different forms of healing that work with the energy of the aura. Although these different forms may have varied underlying philosophies and origins, most energy healing is concerned with cleansing the aura, revitalising the energy and dispelling any residue of imbalance.

In recent years many ancient forms of healing have been rediscovered and adapted to our modern world. A few of the energy-healing techniques available are: Subtle Energy Healing, Seichim, Reiki, Therapeutic Touch, Spiritual Healing, Psychic Healing and Pranic Healing.

Strengthening and refreshing the human aura

As well as indicating an imbalance before illness or disease occurs, the aura may also carry a pattern of imbalance relating to a physical injury or condition that was healed years before.

Our energy systems can also be adversely affected by external influences such as electromagnetic radiation and pollution. Living in an environment where there is less natural, full-spectrum light and fresh air is also a factor.

For this reason, strengthening and refreshing the aura can be very beneficial, and can make us feel more alert and vital. One of the reasons a walk along the beach or through lush forest can be so invigorating is because the air is rich in oxygen and negative ions and cleanses the energy of our auras and chakras.

Importantly, many healers believe that our bodies will heal more quickly and more fully if our energy systems are clear and vibrant.

Strengthening your aura

Taking care of the physical body
Remember that your physical body, your emotional wellbeing and the energy systems of your body are all interrelated. A change in any one of these has an impact on each of the others. So one way to strengthen your aura is to ensure that you are in good physical health.

Some tips towards optimum health are:

- Make sure that you drink plenty of purified or spring water each day – six to eight glasses per day should be your normal intake. This doesn't include water that you consume as coffee, tea or carbonated drinks. Our physical bodies function more efficiently when they are properly hydrated.

- Get some exercise every day, even if it is just a walk in the fresh air. Regular exercise will keep your body in balance. Walking and exercising close to the sea or a large body of water, or in places where there are lots of trees, is the most beneficial, because the oxygen-rich air in these places cleanses your aura while you are toning your physical body. Or perhaps dancing takes your fancy? Dancing without inhibitions will increase your circulation, improve your flexibility and stamina, and release built-up tensions.

- Include an abundance of fresh fruit and vegetables in your diet and avoid highly processed foods – especially those that are high in sodium and fat. Fruit and vegetables gradually lose their vitality after they are harvested, so try to buy them in small amounts and frequently, so that you are eating them at their freshest. Food that retains a lot of its original energy will do more for you than that which has already lost all its life force.

- Rest and relaxation are another two important elements of a lifestyle that will promote a strong and healthy auric body. Fulfilling your work and family responsibilities and living life at a hectic pace eventually take their toll. Do your best to get enough sleep each night, and devote at least half an hour of each day to relaxing in a way that you enjoy.

- Drink alcohol only in moderation. An excessive intake of alcohol will weaken the energy in your system and can leave you feeling depleted. The use of recreational drugs will always weaken the energy system of the body – they are best avoided.

Taking care of your emotional/mental health

Old hurts and unresolved resentments leave energy traces in your aura. Ensuring that you are emotionally healthy will help you maintain a strong and clear aura. Holding on to negative emotions and spending a large portion of your time feeling fearful, jealous or angry can alter the clarity and the colour of your aura.

Seeking the help of professional counsellors, psychotherapists or psychologists can help you gain clarity in the areas of your life that are stressing you or causing you to feel ill at ease.

Depression, for example, is not just an emotional condition – it also impacts on physical health. It is important to seek professional help immediately if you think you may be suffering depression.

Examine, too, the company you keep. If you are in a relationship where you feel that you are always 'giving' but your love, time and attention are not returned, it is very likely that the other person is draining your energy – you may notice that you feel depleted and lacking in energy after spending time with this person. It's important to know whether or not this is a pattern – you may find it easy (or at least possible) to end one relationship because it is 'a one-way street', but, if you repeatedly find yourself in relationships like this, it may be best to seek the help of a therapist to break this behaviour pattern.

An exercise to help strengthen your aura

Our thoughts can have a powerful effect on the energy systems of our body, so we need to learn how to control them and make them work for us – meditation is one of the most effective ways of using our thoughts to strengthen our aura.

The first time you do this exercise, allow at least 45 minutes for it, and choose an environment that is comfortable and where you are unlikely to be disturbed. You will find that once you have become familiar with this exercise you will be able to complete it very quickly in any location.

Begin by closing your eyes and taking a few deep breaths, allowing your attention to stay for a moment on each inward and outward breath. Slowly allow your breathing to fall into its natural rhythm, then take your attention to an area at the very top of your head *(this is the crown chakra, explained in the following chapters)*.

Imagine a beam of gentle, pure white light coming into your body through the top of your head. With each inward breath, imagine more of this light entering your body, and with each outward breath see, in your mind's eye, the light filling every part of your body: first it fills your head, then your chest, shoulders, arms and fingers; then the light fills your torso, down to your hips, thighs, legs, feet and toes.

When your body has become completely filled with this soft white light, imagine the light continuing its journey by moving out through your solar plexus – it moves out of your body and flows around your body, forming a cocoon-like mass. As it encircles you, the very edges of the white light become tinged with pure gold.

As you hold this image in your mind's eye, become aware of the cocoon expanding outwards. When you cannot imagine the cocoon becoming any larger, imagine it shrinking back towards your body until it is only about 25–30 cm (10–12 inches) deep around your body. When you feel ready, gently open your eyes and sit or lie quietly for a few minutes before going on with your day.

Some healers recommend practising this meditation every day, as part of your morning routine. With practice, you will find that you can create your cocoon of white energy within a few moments.

Refreshing and cleansing your aura

There are many ways to cleanse the aura. Remember, intention is a powerful force when dealing with energy, so a meditation in which you imagine your aura cleansed and refreshed can be a simple and effective method of actually cleansing your aura.

Another easy technique is 'brushing down' your energy with your hands. Begin this exercise by setting your intention to cleanse and refresh your auric field. Starting at the top of your head, and with your hands loose but slightly curved, move your hands from the centre of your head outwards, sweeping the energy away from your body. Visualise this old energy around your body moving out of the way to allow fresh, clean, vibrant energy in. Work your way slowly down one side of the body, moving from your head to your neck and shoulders. Sweep the energy away from your chest and torso, then keep your hands moving down, around your legs and to your feet. Repeat the process with the other side of your body. To complete the procedure, use one hand at a time to sweep away the energy around the other arm, then flick the energy away from your hands (as if you're flicking water off your hands).

Cleansing your environment

As you become more aware of the energy fields of your body, you will also become more aware of the energy around you and its impact upon your state of mind. If you are going to take the time to cleanse and strengthen your auric fields, you should give your home and work (if possible) environment an energy spring-cleaning as well.

Cleansing our living environments thoroughly can often take a considerable amount of time, so it's a good idea to set aside at least a couple of days for it. If tackling the whole house at once seems overwhelming, or is impractical, set yourself the task of cleansing one room each week until all the rooms have been cleansed. Once the entire house has been cleansed, you will be amazed at how much easier it is to maintain a clear, clean environment for yourself.

STEP 1
Setting your intention – what outcome would you like from cleansing your environment? Do you want it to be more restful, healthier, more inviting, more nurturing? Set your intention first, so that everything you do to cleanse your environment takes it a step closer to being your ideal space.

STEP 2
Getting rid of clutter – fix what is broken, throw away what cannot be repaired, give away those items you do not use or do not like.

STEP 3
Physical cleaning – it isn't necessary to have your home spotlessly clean at all times (even if that were possible), but part of this cleansing process is that anything that has not been cleaned for a long time or is particularly in need of cleaning should be washed. If it's feasible, leave things to dry in sunshine, as the rays of the sun provide another energy-cleansing process.

STEP 4
Energy cleaning – light an aromatherapy burner (using a mixture of lemon or lemongrass and rosemary essential oils) to clarify the air, and a candle to symbolise light. Open the window (or door) of the room. Stand in a corner of the room, facing the centre of the room. Close your eyes and take a few deep breaths and relax. In your mind, imagine all the energy of the room swirling out the window or door. Repeat this for each corner. When you are standing in the last corner, imagine the room being filled with clear, pure, vibrant energy.

STEP 5
Beautifying – take three items that have special meaning for you, or are simply beautiful, and arrange them so that you will see them every day.

Chakras

What are chakras?

Chakras are the energy centres of the body. A Sanskrit word, 'chakra' means 'wheel' or 'disk', and each chakra moves with a spinning motion, forming a vortex. It is these vortices that filter the energy of the environment around us and disperse it throughout our body. Knowledge of these energy centres is ancient, with its precise origins lost in time – it is generally accepted, though, that the knowledge stems from ancient Hindu teachings.

There are seven major chakras – one enters the physical body at the top of the head, and the other six occur along the vertical midline of the body, with energy entering the body from both the front and the back.

It is important to remember that the chakras are constantly interacting, and that they are no more separate from each other than they are from our aura. Think in terms of the chakras being an intense concentration of energy within our entire energy system. Although the energy moving through the chakras is always moving, the vitality of the energy can lessen if an area of our life is out of balance.

Western cultures generally believe that our behaviour and our actions are largely governed by our intellect. In Eastern cultures, the idea that the movement of energy into and around our bodies influences our state of mind – and therefore our actions – is well known. These energy channels are also considered part of our connection with the divine, with a higher consciousness.

There are many exercises, meditations and healing techniques that focus on 'balancing the chakras', and aim to help us remove any blocks or imbalances to the natural movement of energy. It is believed that when the energy of the chakras is flowing freely and operating as an integrated whole, we will operate at our optimum level of physical, emotional and spiritual wellbeing.

The inner energy of the seven chakras

First chakra

The meaning of the Sanskrit name of the first chakra, Muladhara, is 'root', and it is this first chakra that acts as our root, and is concerned with our connection to the earth and our very basic, fundamental needs for survival – sustenance, shelter, the health of our physical body and safety.

If the energy of this chakra is depleted or blocked, our connection to nature and the world around us may be weakened. As a result, we are likely to feel 'spacey' or 'ungrounded', and less stable. In this condition, we may neglect our physical needs, and we may become unhealthy and weak as a result of this neglect.

If the energy of this chakra is overstimulated, we may become too attached to things of the physical world, and place too much importance on material wealth and possessions. We may be unable to develop the 'higher' levels of our nature because we are afraid to risk losing these possessions. A miser, a person who is unable to enjoy their wealth for fear of losing it, is the perfect example of the energy of this chakra being out of balance.

This chakra is often referred to as the 'base' chakra.

The first chakra is located:
At the base of the spine

The corresponding colour
to this chakra is: Red

The Sanskrit name of this chakra is:
Muladhara

Commonly referred to as the:
Base chakra

This chakra is represented by:
A lotus of four petals

Second chakra

The energy of the second chakra is concerned with change, with creating form from formlessness. Our creativity, whether it is expressed artistically, academically, physically or in the ultimate creative act –producing a child – is the energy of the second chakra. Second chakra energy is also the source of our sexuality. A free flow of energy through this chakra will be manifested as vitality and a passionate approach to life.

The Sanskrit name of this chakra roughly translates as 'to sweeten', as the energy of this chakra is concerned with the pleasures of life, with desires and with nurturing ourselves and our creativity. When it is in balance, this chakra brings an immense amount of pleasure into our lives. It allows us to see the beauty in the people and things around us, and allows us to take delight in our own creative abilities and passions.

If we have an excess of energy in this chakra, we may be overly focused on satisfying our desires, or unaware or unwilling to acknowledge that it is not always necessary or healthy to have all our desires met. If we have depleted energy levels in this chakra, we may deprive ourselves of any pleasure, or try to deny that we have any desires, and thus stifle our creativity and our passion.

This chakra is often referred to as the 'sacral', 'belly' or 'spleen' chakra.

The second chakra is located:
In the lower abdomen

The corresponding colour to this chakra is: Orange

The Sanskrit name of this chakra is: Svadhisthana

Commonly referred to as the: Sacral chakra

This chakra is represented by: A lotus of six petals

Third chakra

The energy of the third chakra is concerned with personal power. Our sense of our place in the world, our confidence in ourselves, and our self-esteem are centred on this chakra. It is the seat of our will. Our ability to stand by our convictions and carry out what we have willed is dependent on the energy of this chakra.

With this chakra out of balance, we may be overly sensitive to the reactions of other people, feeling indifference or coolness as rejection, and anything less than totally positive feedback as criticism of ourselves. Our 'inner critic' may also be operating at a level where we have little confidence in our capabilities, our worthiness or our chances of being loved.

When this chakra is in balance, we are able to accept the responsibilities that are truly ours and be confident in our actions and abilities. We are able to decide how we wish to act and then maintain our chosen courses of action. We will also be able to function without the approval of everyone around us. The courage and strength to be who we are without outside approval is a sign of healthy self-esteem.

This chakra is often referred to as the 'solar plexus' or 'navel' chakra.

The third chakra is located: At the solar plexus

The corresponding colour to this chakra is: Yellow

The Sanskrit name of this chakra is: Manipura

Commonly referred to as the: Solar Plexus chakra

This chakra is represented by: A lotus of 10 petals

Fourth chakra

The fourth chakra is concerned with unconditional love. It affects our ability to consider others, to be gentle in our expectations of ourselves and to empathise with the challenges and the joys experienced by others. It is the link between our intellect and our spiritual selves.

Unconditional love is a state of being – it can also be a conscious decision. We can engage our will (the third chakra) and direct the love of the fourth chakra to all those around us. When we are aware of how all things are interconnected, and give unconditional love to all those around us, we have a great sense of inner peace and wellbeing.

A person who is continually giving, even when they are in need themselves, is likely to be out of balance in third chakra energy *(see page 52)*. Similarly, someone who denies any empathy with those around them and is unable to show compassion would likely have depleted energy in the fourth chakra.

This chakra is often referred to as the 'heart' chakra.

The fourth chakra is located:
In the middle of the chest

The corresponding colour to this chakra is: Green

The Sanskrit name of this chakra is: Anahata

Commonly referred to as the:
Heart chakra

This chakra is represented by:
A lotus of 12 petals

Fifth chakra

Expression and communication, both verbal and non-verbal, are the themes of the fifth chakra. Some mystics believe that the throat chakra is responsible for the telepathic abilities that are often associated with 'picking up' on the thoughts of others. You may be experiencing these abilities when you know that the phone is about to ring before it does, or when you know who is on the phone before you answer a call. From an energy viewpoint, this kind of telepathy is possible because every living thing is connected by the energy that flows through the chakras.

When this chakra is in balance, we are considered and thoughtful with our communications, and aware of how they affect those around us. We are able to express our needs and our desires, and maintain tour personal integrity with our communications – to 'speak our truth' without being hurtful to others.

When this chakra is out of balance, we are likely to be over-talkative, and to speak about nothing in particular. In this state, it is very difficult for us to listen, and those around us are unlikely to spend very long listening to us. When we have depleted energy in this chakra, we are likely to be uncommunicative, or we give unclear messages in our non-verbal communications.

This chakra is often referred to as the 'throat' chakra.

The fifth chakra is located:
At the throat

The corresponding colour to this chakra is: Blue

The Sanskrit name of this chakra is: Visuddha

Commonly referred to as the: Throat chakra

This chakra is represented by: A lotus of 16 petals

Sixth chakra

The third eye is the chakra where the conscious meets the unconscious, where our imagination and inner 'sight' reside. The development of this chakra involves becoming more aware of our intuition and extrasensory perception. This is the energy of clairvoyance, and of other abilities such as precognition (the ability to know of an event before it happens) and psychometry (the ability to 'sense' information about an event or a person by touching or holding a related object).

An excess of energy in this chakra can mean that a person will be too influenced by the psychic realm, and may become 'ungrounded', disorganised or disoriented, and appear 'spacey'. A depletion of sixth chakra energy can lead to a person being seen as narrow-minded and fixed in their thinking. They may be uncomfortable with anything that challenges them to think or feel something beyond their usual 'tunnel vision'.

If we have a balanced sixth chakra, we can utilise this additional information and combine it with our innate wisdom in order to make decisions that are not based on fear or ego. We are able to use our minds and the power of visualisation to have a positive impact on our surroundings and to improve the quality of our lives and the lives of those around us.

This chakra is often referred to as the 'brow' or 'third eye' chakra.

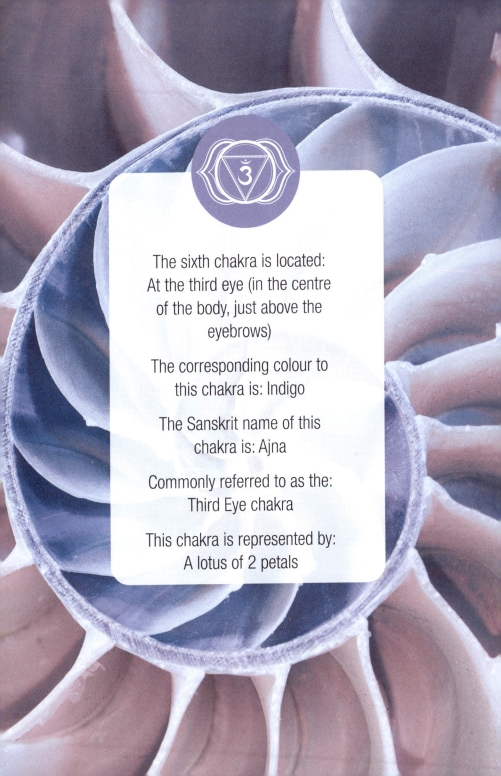

The sixth chakra is located:
At the third eye (in the centre of the body, just above the eyebrows)

The corresponding colour to this chakra is: Indigo

The Sanskrit name of this chakra is: Ajna

Commonly referred to as the: Third Eye chakra

This chakra is represented by: A lotus of 2 petals

Seventh chakra

The seventh chakra is about insight, inner 'knowing', and self-realisation. It is the home of our spirituality and our connection with the divine. The Sanskrit name for this chakra means 'thousandfold', referring to the number of petals of the lotus that represents this chakra. It symbolises the unlimited nature of our thought processes.

This chakra is the portal through which the energy that is the human life force enters the body. From the seventh chakra, this energy filters down through every other part of the body and through each of the other chakras. The strength and vitality of this energy in a person reflects their level of personal development.

Developed to its full potential, the energy of this chakra brings the highest level of consciousness, and is an indication that the person has mastered the challenges of all the other chakras.

Many healers and mystics believe that humankind, as part of the evolutionary process, is moving toward an ever larger number of people who are fully developing this chakra. When the majority of people have developed the crown chakra, it is expected that humankind will take a great step forward, away from the needs and conflicts of the lower chakras toward a more spiritually oriented existence.

This chakra is often referred to as the 'crown' or 'coronal' chakra.

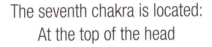

The seventh chakra is located:
At the top of the head

The corresponding colour to this chakra is: Violet

The Sanskrit name of this chakra is: Sahasrara

Commonly referred to as the: Crown chakra

This chakra is represented by: A lotus of 1000 petals

Minor chakras

Although the seven chakras are by far the major energy centres of the body, there are additional minor chakras – at the hands, the feet and the knees. Some researchers have claimed up to 122 secondary chakras. Some mystics also recognise a chakra located below the feet, connecting us to the earth, and another located approximately 30 cm (12 inches) above the crown chakra, connecting us to the divine.

Chakras in the hands

To feel the energy centres in your hands, begin by clenching your hands into fists a few times. Then relax your hands and, positioning your hands about 30 cm (12 inches) apart, very gradually move your hands closer together. You may be able to feel an increased 'pressure' between your hands – this is the energy of the minor chakras in your hands. People who practise energy-healing techniques often feel quite intense heat flowing from their hands during and after healing sessions, as their hand chakras are activated.

The chakras and our personal growth

The journey through the chakras can be seen as a reflection of our personal journey of growth and self-awareness. As we grow and develop, the focus of our lives incorporates the energy of each successive chakra.

First chakra – survival instincts

The first chakra is about our survival. Do I have enough food, water and money to survive? Do I have shelter? Am I physically safe?

The first chakra represents the very base level of existence for us, and reveals our most instinctive selves. Our strongest instinct is to survive, and so, until we are confident that these basics of wellbeing are in place and believe that they will always be available to us, survival will tend to dominate our thoughts and drive our actions.

This doesn't mean that we cannot achieve personal growth unless we become wealthy. It is often more a matter of trusting that our world is an abundant place and that all we need is available to us.

It is also important to recognise that our basic needs are under threat at all times (from events such as losing a job or losing a large amount of money through an unwise investment); our instinct for survival will take over if it is needed.

Balance in this chakra means making sure that our basic physical needs are met without these needs becoming an obsession.

From an evolutionary perspective, early man's hunting and gathering is very much focused on the energy of the base chakra. Our modern society is much less focused on this level of energy than the very first societies, for whom life revolved almost entirely around the collection of food, finding shelter and avoiding danger.

Second chakra – pleasures, desires and creation

Beyond our immediate need for survival, our second chakra is concerned with desires, with sexuality and with the act of creation. From the perspective of personal growth, this chakra, too, is very much an instinctive energy.

How the energy is developed in this chakra may dictate whether we deprive ourselves of the pleasures of life or follow our desires with such ferociousness that they become addictions, then providing us with very little pleasure.

Balance in the second chakra means that we neither deny ourselves pleasure nor overindulge in pleasures that may be detrimental to our health and wellbeing. When this chakra is in balance, we feel able to express our sexuality in ways that are empowering to our lovers and ourselves. Balance means that we can also readily access our creativity, and can find many ways of expressing this creativity in our work and play.

From an evolutionary perspective, the second chakra energy came into operation with humankind's realisation that, by operating as a community rather than as individuals, we could achieve more and make our survival easier. When people settled in one place and began to operate as groups, sacral chakra energy was in operation.

Third chakra – relating to the world around us

Our sense of personal power, of having choice in our actions – without the need to feel power over another person – comes as our third chakra is opened and in balance. With the awakening of this chakra comes the realisation that we have power over our lives. Although we cannot control every event in our lives, we can shape our futures and the directions our lives take by accepting this responsibility and consciously directing our actions.

Balance in the third chakra means that we neither seek to overpower others nor allow others to disempower us. We are able to step beyond the circumstances where we feel we have been victims of other people's actions, or of events beyond our control, and change our perceptions of ourselves.

From an evolutionary perspective, the world is still in third chakra energy. The industrial revolution and subsequent advances in technology have radically changed the lives of many, and allowed more people to pursue personal endeavours, but conflicts and power struggles between different communities and between different countries are still resolved through violence and war.

Fourth chakra – love

When our ability to take responsibility for our actions is firmly established, we are then able to express love without our own needs, fears and desires being the motivating factors. Where the second chakra relates to love in terms of sexual expression, the fourth chakra relates to a conscious choice to act with love towards ourselves and those around us. This type of love does not require anyone to change in order to be worthy of receiving it.

When we have fully integrated the energy of this chakra, we can recognise that holding onto hurts and grievances benefits no one, least of all ourselves. We find it easy to forgive and to release the emotional pain we experience as part of everyday life.

Balance in this chakra means that we are able to give and receive unconditional love, and our actions are based on the premise that all people are deserving of love.

Fifth chakra – effective communication

To communicate effectively, we need to be empathic – to be able to really listen to what another person is saying, and try to understand it from their perspective. We cannot be empathic if, while we are listening, we are also filtering what is being said through our own prejudices, inadequacies and fears.

Effective communication also involves being able to express ourselves without seeking the approval or agreement of the person we are speaking with. We need to be able to 'speak our truth' without requiring a particular reaction or response in order to feel acceptable. If this chakra is out of balance, others may see us as arrogant and self-righteous, allowing little space for the opinions or views of others. Depleted energy in this area may mean that we find it difficult to express ourselves or make ourselves understood.

Balance in this chakra means that we are able to hear and be heard without past emotional hurts or current fears and feelings of shame affecting what we say and what we hear.

Sixth chakra – imagination and inspiration

Rediscovering our imagination and allowing ourselves to tune into our intuitive nature are the gifts of the sixth chakra. At some point along the path of personal development, most of us will recognise that we have access to a far greater wisdom than we ever realised. As our personal development continues, we are increasingly able to make judgements and decisions based on what we 'know' to be true without needing to have a rational or logical explanation for our 'knowledge'.

Listening to our intuition can be difficult at first, because education, at least in the Western world, is based almost entirely on facts and logic. There is little room in this system for developing our intuition. Facts are either right or wrong, and an argument or line of thought is either logical or illogical. Intuition, on the other hand, is neither right nor wrong, neither logical nor illogical – it simply 'is'.

Balance in this chakra allows us to connect fully to our intuition, and confidently make decisions based on the information we gain from this.

Seventh chakra – knowledge and spiritual enlightenment

An imbalance in this chakra may present itself as mental instability, with an excess of energy resulting in episodes of manic or psychotic behaviour. Without self-awareness and balance, excess energy in this chakra can also express itself as a drive to collect possessions and material wealth, and to build a sense of personal power.

Depleted energy in this chakra may generate feelings of despondency and depression, with the person having little drive or energy to make choices and take direction in their lives. Following someone else's dictates without thinking or challenging them becomes the easiest option. Eventually, a person like this may feel a complete lack of any sense of personal power.

Balance in this chakra leads to what has been described by yoga adepts as a 'blissful' and 'ecstatic' state. This is the final stage of evolution of the physical body, and it brings with it a sense of inner peace, access to our innate wisdom, and understanding and awareness of our connection with all other living things. In this state, we are able to recognise within ourselves any patterns of thoughts and behaviours that are dysfunctional, and effortlessly release them from our psyche.

Chakras and Kundalini

Kundalini is an energy force that may spontaneously rise from the base chakra, moving through the chakras and activating each as it ascends. The Kundalini eventually makes its way to the crown chakra, causing an opening and expansion of that chakra. In traditional teachings, the rising of the Kundalini is thought to be triggered by – or the result of – an increase in spiritual understanding and consciousness.

Those who practise yoga may consciously focus on encouraging the Kundalini energy to rise up the spine by using certain postures, purification rituals and breathing techniques. They may also choose to follow a guru or spiritual teacher, in the belief that the spiritual enlightenment of the teacher may be passed on to them.

The rising of the Kundalini may also occur spontaneously. Some say this rising feels as if a serpent is uncoiling from the base chakra and intensifying the activity of each chakra as it rises.

For some, the process of Kundalini has been described as happening in a moment; others may experience this intense movement of energy over weeks or months.

The serpent Goddess Kundalini

In ancient Hindu mythology, the Goddess Kundalini, one incarnation of the Great Mother deities, was represented as a serpent sleeping coiled at the base of the spine.

As a symbol of our connection to the Divine Feminine, the energy of Kundalini lies waiting at the base chakra. For the soul to fulfil its highest potential, the Kundalini energy must rise upwards through the chakras towards the Divine Masculine of the crown chakra. This union of the feminine and masculine is also the joining of the creative and the sexual energies.

Healing with chakras

Each of the chakras relates to particular parts of the body, and an imbalance in the energy of a particular chakra may mean that the related areas may be more susceptible to illness and disease. If we understand the nature of the energy of each chakra, it may be possible to support physical healing by examining the emotional/mental/energy aspects of the corresponding chakra.

For example, ailments or illnesses involving the digestive system relate to the solar plexus chakra. The energy of the solar plexus chakra is based around personal power, so the questions to be asked are 'Am I feeling a lack of personal power in some area of my life?' and 'Am I abusing my personal power in some way?' Meditating on these questions may bring some insight into why this area of the body is out of balance.

This is not, of course, a replacement for medical assistance – qualified care should be sought for any illness or condition.

Base chakra: Legs, feet and skeletal system. This chakra also relates to the muscle tissue of the body and to the immune system. It corresponds to the adrenal glands.

Sacral chakra: Kidneys, bladder, genitals and the uterus. It corresponds to the ovaries and testes.

Solar plexus chakra: Digestive system and lower back. It corresponds to the pancreas gland.

Heart chakra: Lungs and heart. It corresponds to the thymus gland.

Throat chakra: Neck, shoulders and arms. It corresponds to the thyroid gland.

Third eye chakra: Eyes.
It corresponds to the pituitary gland.

Crown chakra: Central nervous system. It corresponds to the pineal gland.

The flow of energy through the chakras

Healers who work with energy and are sensitive to the energy of the chakras are often aware of the spinning movement of the chakras – the speed and evenness of the spinning are used to gauge whether or not the chakra is in balance. When the entire energy system of the chakras is integrated and balanced, energy flows smoothly and freely between them:

- The first (base) chakra moves in a clockwise direction and connects to the physical auric body.

- The second (sacral) chakra moves in an anticlockwise direction and connects to the etheric auric body.

- The third (solar plexus) chakra moves in a clockwise direction and connects to the vital auric body.

- The fourth (heart) chakra moves in an anticlockwise direction and connects to the astral auric body or the Emotional Aura.

- The fifth (throat) chakra moves in a clockwise direction and connects to the lower mental auric body.

- The sixth (third eye) chakra moves in an anticlockwise direction and connects to the higher mental auric body.

- The seventh (crown) chakra moves in a clockwise direction and connects to the spiritual auric body.

Focusing on balance

Although healers may often refer to 'opening' a chakra or 'unblocking' a chakra, there is always energy moving through these energy centres. The real aim is balance in the amount and the flow of energy through the chakras.

There are many ways to help balance our chakras. There are physical exercises to strengthen the body *(see the next section)* and in turn the strength of the energy flowing through the body; there are also therapies such as flower essences and aromatherapy oils; and there are many other subtle energy-healing techniques.

Emotional wellbeing also affects the energy of the chakras — clearing the residue of our emotional disturbances will increase the vitality of our energy systems.

Strengthening the physical body

Base chakra exercises

Walking is one of the best base chakra exercises. The connection you make with the ground with each step helps balance the first chakra's energy while strengthening and toning your legs and respiratory system.

Choose places of beauty and fresh air to take long walks. Start with slow, gentle walks; as your fitness improves, increase the pace and the length of your stride. Carry a small backpack with some water and a high-energy snack in case you are inspired to walk further than usual, and don't forget to also take in the beauty of the surroundings.

Sacral chakra exercises

Dancing to strong, rhythmic music is a wonderful release for the sacral chakra. Many traditional and indigenous cultures have a wealth of music that is ideally suited to sacral chakra dancing. African drumming can be particularly powerful because of the strength of its complex rhythms. If you are not used to dancing, or you have not danced for a long time, you might like to begin dancing by yourself, so that you can feel the freedom of moving your body without also feeling self-conscious.

Don't worry about dancing in a particular style – just let your body do whatever it feels like doing, and improvise with moving your hips and pelvis. Have the music loud enough for you to be able to 'lose' yourself in the repetitive sounds.

Solar plexus chakra exercises

This exercise is sometimes known as 'the cat', and it is particularly good for the energy of the third chakra. You may like to incorporate it with some other stretching exercise, working on either a yoga mat or on a carpet or rug. On a physical level, this exercise helps tone the muscles of the waist and increases the suppleness of the spine.

> STEP 1
> Position yourself on your hands and knees, with your palms flat on the floor, arms straight and shoulder-width apart, legs hip-width apart, back parallel with the floor, and your thighs at a right angle to the floor.
>
> STEP 2
> Breathe slowly and deeply, then on the exhale, bring your back upward and your head down towards your chest. Take your chin as close to your chest as you can, and hold it there for a few moments.
>
> STEP 3
> Now slowly breathe in, letting your back sink down, and raise your head to look up at the ceiling. Hold this position for a few moments.
>
> STEP 4
> Repeat steps 2 and 3 four or five times.

Heart chakra exercises

Any exercise that helps expand the chest will also help free the energy of the fourth chakra. One of the easiest – and perhaps the most enjoyable – exercises for this is to sing. Breathing deeply into the diaphragm (the diaphragm is between your lungs and your stomach) while you sing and letting your voice flow effortlessly from your body is a great way to expand the chest area.

If you already sing a lot, it will be no surprise to you that singing will also make you feel great. If you don't sing regularly, don't be concerned with whether you are singing 'correctly' or in tune or whether you sound 'good' or not. Sing in the shower if this is your only opportunity to sing without feeling self-conscious.

Throat chakra exercises

The areas of the body influenced by the fifth chakra are the neck, throat and jaw. Physically, the neck is the bridge between the head and the body. Symbolically, it is the link between thought and action. As this area deals with contradictions, it is not uncommon for there to be a great amount of tension here.

A self-massage of the neck area with a small amount of oil or body lotion is simple and quick. If you do it often, it can be very beneficial in reducing stress.

Sit on the floor, in a chair, or lie with your back on the floor with your knees bent and your feet flat on the floor.

STEP 1
Using your right hand, stroke from the bottom of your skull, down the left side of your neck to your shoulder, then over your shoulder and down your arm to your elbow. Glide your hand gently back to the base of the skull and repeat two or three times.

STEP 2
With your right hand, using gentle kneading movements, work from your neck down to your wrist. Gently glide your hand back to your neck and repeat.

STEP 3
Use small, circular movements with the pads of your fingers and apply gentle pressure to work deeply into the muscles. Begin at the back of your neck, beside the spine, and work out towards the side of the neck and down to your shoulder.

STEP 4
Repeat steps 1, 2 and 3 using your left hand on the right side of your body.

Third eye chakra exercises

Walking meditations are an excellent exercise for both the body and the third eye chakra, as are other physical exercises where the mind is actively engaged in the activity. Rock climbing and gymnastics are examples of strenuous third eye chakra exercises; hatha yoga or tai chi are more gentle choices.

Crown chakra exercises

One of the classic yoga positions for the crown chakra is the headstand. Unless you have a relatively high degree of flexibility and/or the guidance of a yoga teacher, the headstand can be a little confronting.

You can, however, achieve a similar effect by using a tilt-board (where your feet are higher than your head) at the gym or at home, or by raising one end of your bed or a massage table. Do not stay in this position for more than three to four minutes at first, but increase the time gradually over a few weeks.

Health benefits are said to include improved circulation and relief of lower back pain.

Warning: if you have a heart condition, high blood pressure or any eye condition, please do not undertake any of these exercises without medical supervision.

Clearing emotional disturbances

Unresolved traumas, stresses and emotional upsets leave a residue within the energy system of your body. A small argument, where you don't feel too threatened or hurt, may clear reasonably quickly from your energy system, but an upset where you feel deeply affected, or where you feel that many issues remain unresolved, may leave long-lasting remnants in your energy system. *See 'Taking care of your emotional/mental health', (page 42)* for more information on how to ensure that your energy system is not clogged with past hurts and grievances.

Harnessing the power of the chakras

To harness the power of the chakras is to fully integrate the energy of each chakra into your life. One way to do this is to undertake a seven-week programme to increase your awareness of each chakra.

You are likely to gain more insights into your nature, and into whether or not there is balance in your chakras, if you keep a journal of this process. Through the act of writing down your thoughts, your experiences, your daydreams and your fears, you will make connections between seemingly isolated incidents that occur during the seven weeks. 'Aha' moments, where you will understand a pattern of behaviour you were previously unaware of, often come through this process of writing.

Don't make the journal a chore; just keep it close at hand and add to it when you feel inspired. Allow your creativity to flow – use coloured pens or pencils and add doodles or drawings as you go. Include things you've read or things people have said that have moved you.

Seven week programme

Week 1 — Focus on the base chakra

In this week, be especially aware of your most basic needs and how well you are taking care of them. Are you nurturing yourself on this level? Below are some aspects of your daily routine you can examine.

- Are you eating nutritious, balanced meals with lots of fresh fruit and vegetables?
- Are you getting enough undisturbed sleep?
- Is some form of gentle exercise part of your daily routine?
- Is your health fundamentally sound?
- Do you feel financially secure? If not, what can you do to improve your situation?

Make a list of things that you can do this week that will help you support yourself with your basic needs. Gradually make these things habits.

Week 2 — Focus on the sacral chakra

Treat yourself to sensual experiences in this week. Choose things that will delight you, and that immediately appeal to you. Make sure you do something that awakens your enthusiasm and your imagination every day. Below are some ideas for sensual experiences.

- Take a long, scented bubble bath and allow yourself time to soak and relax.
- Go to a performance of chamber music or a choral recital.
- Visit an art gallery with some pastels and a sketch pad and create your own interpretation of your favourite painting.
- Book yourself an aromatherapy massage.
- Take a gentle, ambling walk through a forest or by the sea.
- Make your favourite meal and your favourite dessert.

Week 3 — Focus on the solar plexus chakra

Our will is a powerful tool, but one that we are never taught to use. When you do the following exercise, you may find that you add something to it each day, refining your vision as you become more confident.

Write down how you would like your life to be. Include answers to the following questions, but try to make sure that you are not listing what you think others around you expect of you. Look within yourself to find the answers, and focus on what you truly want.

Where do you live? Are you in a relationship? What is that relationship like? How much money do you earn? What type of work do you do? How many hours a week do you work? What type of friends do you have?

Each day of this week, take a few moments to repeat the following affirmations several times – they will help your self-esteem.

- 'I treat myself with respect, love and compassion.'
- 'I deserve the very best in life: joy, happiness, love and prosperity.'
- 'I choose, today and every day, how I will think and how I will behave.'

Week 4 — Focus on the heart chakra

This week, make a list of all the people you feel angry at or hurt by – go as far back as you can remember.

Take a few moments to calm your mind and bring your attention to your breath. Now imagine the first person on the list and the incident that caused you to feel angry and/or hurt. See if you can understand their behaviour. Were they themselves feeling angry, hurt, threatened or fearful?

Acknowledge that you would prefer them to have acted differently, but also that you have survived this incident and that it only holds as much power over you as you allow. Make a conscious decision to forgive this person.

Imagine each incident as a handful of sand. Let each one slip through your fingers, as you no longer need to hold onto the hurt/anger associated with it.

When you are ready, move onto the next person on the list.

Week 5 — Focus on the throat chakra

The challenge for this week is to listen for the true meaning in the words of those around you.

Pay attention to everyone's body language and tone of voice, so that you really 'hear' what they are saying. Allow a pause between listening and speaking yourself, to ensure that the other person has finished what they needed to say before you speak.

Respond to each person by openly and honestly expressing yourself. In practice, this will mean setting aside 'chit chat' and being more conscious of what you are saying.

This is more challenging than it sounds. If at first you find it too difficult to do this constantly, try to do it for half an hour, then for 45 minutes, then gradually increase the time. You will soon find that you are expressing yourself in this way, and listening in this way, without even thinking about it.

Week 6 — Focus on the third eye chakra

This week, pay particular attention to your intuition and, when you make a decision, listen first for your inner voice.

It takes practice to pay attention to this voice, as we often disregard information we receive from our intuition and only realise after the event that we 'knew' we should have made a different choice. It also takes some practice to discern what is intuition and what comes from other inner voices, voices that are driven by fears or insecurities, or by the ego. Take a few chances and follow the guidance of your intuition.

The third eye chakra is also related to your spirituality, so, if you follow the teachings of a religion, you may like to take some extra time this week to attend the spiritual services of your faith. If the idea appeals to you, you may also like to attend the services of another religion and listen to the messages of that faith with an open mind and heart.

Week 7 — Focus on the crown chakra

This week is a time to reflect on and integrate the results of the previous six weeks of this programme.

Read through your journal and reflect on what you have learned about yourself — and what you may have rediscovered. At this point you will have a clearer picture of who you are, what you want in life, and which patterns of behaviour you want to release.

Each day of this week, spend at least 15 minutes in meditation or quiet contemplation on one aspect of the previous weeks. End each meditation with the affirmations listed below.

- 'I release all thoughts and actions that limit my self-awareness.'
- 'I acknowledge that I have unlimited potential and that I have access to all knowledge.'
- 'Without any need to change, I am who I am, unique and perfect.'

Chakras and sound

Each chakra also has a corresponding sound, and one way to clear the energy of the chakras is to voice these sounds while focusing on the corresponding area of the body. It is important to note at this point that we are all individuals, and each of our cells and each of our chakras is unique to us. When using sound, trust your intuition and what feels 'easy' and 'right'. Ease and richness in the sound you produce is the best indication that you are producing a sound that is resonating with your chakras.

Like most pursuits in life, you will find creating the sounds for the chakras easier with practice – at first you may find that the sounds you create are a little 'thin', or that your voice breaks easily. Don't be concerned by this. Simply take a deep breath, and, on exhaling, imagine tension leaving your body. Then begin again.

Take a few moments to get comfortable. You may decide to sit on the floor with your legs crossed, or in a chair with your feet flat on the floor – just make sure your spine is straight and your shoulders are relaxed. Take a few deep breaths, allowing your focus to move inward from the outside world to the rhythmic pattern of your own breathing.

Commencing with the base chakra, make the sound 'oo' – there is no set length of time to maintain the toning, simply stop when it feels right to do so. You may like to sit in silence for a few moments before you start to make the sound that corresponds to the sacral chakra, and before you continue on upward through the chakras.

Don't be surprised or concerned if you feel a welling of emotion while you are toning *(see page 92)* – your emotions are as connected to your energy centres as your physical body is.

Toning and the chakras

Toning is a simple healing technique that requires no musical aptitude or experience, and no previous singing experience – everyone can tone. Your toning will be a reflection of your physical, emotional and energy state.

Toning means creating elongated vowel sounds with your voice. There is no set pitch for the sounds – if you experiment with creating vowel sounds at different pitches, you will know when a particular pitch 'resonates' with the area of the body you're toning to. For each chakra, you will find that one particular pitch 'feels right', and is the easiest to maintain.

Experiment, too, with the loudness of your toning – with some sounds you may wish to tone as loudly as you can, while with other sounds you may need to tone more softly. Trust your intuition in regard to how long you tone to any one chakra.

Chakra balancing toning exercise
This exercise needs three (or more) people to be most effective. The person who is to have their chakras balanced should lie on the floor or on a massage table. For comfort, place a small cushion or pillow under the person's head and knees.

The other two people stand or kneel on either side of the person, facing one another, level with the person's base chakra. Each person should set their intention on balancing the chakras of the person on the floor or massage table. Starting softly, the two 'toners' should begin toning 'uuhh', gently moderating the tone until they feel that the sound they are creating is in harmony and is resonating across the person's body. Interestingly, both toners will often stop toning simultaneously, without the need for either to signal an end.

The toners should then gradually work up the body towards the head, toning each chakra with its corresponding sounds (or another sound if their intuition indicates that it is appropriate). At the end of the chakra balancing, the toners and receiver may wish to sit in silence for a few moments before changing roles.

The sounds of the chakras

Base chakra
oo (like the vowel sound in 'loot')

Sacral chakra
oh (like the vowel sound in 'mow')

Solar plexus chakra
aw (like the vowel sound in 'door')

Heart chakra
ay (like the vowel sound in 'hay')

Throat chakra
eh (like the vowel sound in 'feather')

Third eye chakra
ih (like the vowel sound in 'in')

Crown chakra
ee (like the vowel sound in 'bee')

Chakra exercises and meditations

Chakra meditation with music

Each chakra has a music note that its energy resonates with. Working from the base chakra upwards to the crown, these notes are: C, D, E, F, G, A and B. In her book *Sounding the Inner Landscape*, Kay Gardner also attributes to each chakra a 'balancing' or complementary note that is a musical fifth above the chakra's main note (i.e., G, A, B, C, D, E and F#).

There are many recordings of music that has been written specifically for working with the chakras – music that takes the notes of all the chakras and weaves them into a single piece.

The following are recordings for chakra meditation with music:

- *Chakra Suite* by Steven Halpern
- *Chakra Chants* by Jonathan Goldman
- *The Seven Chakra System* by Remko Arentz
- *Chakra Meditation Music* by Merlin's Magic
- *Tibetan Chakra Meditations* by Ben Scott
- *Chakra Dance* by Malcolm Stern

You may also wish to create your own 'moving meditations' or improvised dance to pieces of music that you intuitively feel relate to particular chakras. For example, many people feel that cello pieces such as J.S. Bach's *Brandenburg Concertos* resonate with the heart chakra, while Gregorian Chants from the Abbey of Solesmes in France resonate with the brow and crown chakras.

Breathing visualisation

Using breathing with visualisation can help create balance in our energy system; add colour as well, for maximum impact.

Sit or lie comfortably and allow your breathing to become slow and smooth. Release as much tension as you can from your head, neck and shoulders.

Now, imagine that in front of you there is a mist of deep red. As you take in two or three deep breaths, your mouth and lungs fill with this rich colour. As you take a few more deep breaths, the red moves through and down your body, spiralling out the front and back of your body through the base chakra.

Repeat this process with the other chakras: breathe in orange, and breathe it out through the sacral chakra; breathe in yellow, and breathe it out through the solar plexus chakra; breathe in green, and breathe it out through the heart chakra; breathe in blue, and breathe it out through the throat chakra; breathe in indigo, and breathe it out through the third eye chakra; and finally, breathe in violet, and breathe this out through the crown chakra.